INSECTS

INSECTS

MICHAEL GEORGE

THE CHILD'S WORLD

DESIGN
Bill Foster of Albarella & Associates, Inc.

PHOTO CREDITS
Robert & Linda Mitchell: front cover, back cover,
13 (top and bottom), 21, 23, 31
Doug Wechsler/VIREO: 9, 15, 25, 29
COMSTOCK/Townsend Dickinson: 2
COMSTOCK/Jack Clark: 11, 17
COMSTOCK/George Lepp: 19, 27

Distributed to schools and libraries
in the United States by
ENCYCLOPAEDIA BRITANNICA EDUCATIONAL CORP
310 South Michigan Ave.
Chicago, Illinois 60604

Library of Congress Cataloging-in-Publication Data
George, Michael, 1964-
Insects/Michael George.
p. cm. — (Child's World Wildlife Library)
Summary: Describes the characteristics and behavior of
such insects as the army ant, cockroach, and firefly.
ISBN 0-89565-703-1

1. Insects — Juvenile literature.   [1. Insects.]   I. Title.
II. Series.   91-13373
QL467.2.G47 1991   CIP
595.7—dc20   AC

CONTENTS

For most people, insects are annoying pests they would like to live without. Ants raid our picnics, mosquitoes suck our blood, and termites destroy our homes. Although some species are pests, insects are important members of the wildlife community. They help break down dead animals, pollinate plants, and provide food for many forms of life.

Scientists have identified about 1 million different kinds of insects. Insects fly through the sky, run across the ground, crawl beneath the soil, and even skate on the ocean. With so many different species living in so many different places, insects are the most successful group of animals on the planet.

All insects have bodies that are divided into three parts: the head, the thorax, and the abdomen. Insects also have three pairs of legs, and many have wings. Although all insects share these features, each species has unique characteristics that help it survive in its particular environment. As a result, insects vary greatly in size, appearance, and way of life. The following are some of the fascinating insects that live on the planet earth.

ARMY ANT

There are about 14,000 kinds of ants in the world. Although most of these species are harmless, army ants of Central and South America are a notable exception. Army ants live in colonies that contain thousands of members. Each morning, the colonies march through tropical forests in search of food. These ants prefer live game to family picnics. Gaining power in numbers, the ants swarm over insects, lizards, rodents, or even larger animals if they cannot escape. Bit by bit, the tiny insects tear their victims to pieces. By sunset, the ants are off in search of fresh hunting grounds.

MOSQUITO

Mosquitoes live throughout the world, from the frozen polar regions to the sunny tropics. Their vast numbers, combined with their irritating bites, make mosquitoes one of the most disliked insects on the planet. Surprisingly, male mosquitoes cannot be blamed for the annoying bites. They feed only on the nectar of flowers. Female mosquitoes, however, depend on blood for important nutrients. With syringelike beaks, they pierce the skin of humans and other animals, then suck up their meal of blood. The female's saliva causes the familiar irritation of a mosquito bite.

FIREFLY

Fireflies are peculiar creatures. On warm summer nights, they make forests and meadows twinkle with flashing lights. The flashes are caused by chemical reactions inside the firefly's body. Each type of firefly gives off a particular color of light. The colors range from bright yellow to tints of blue, green, or red. The firefly's signals are meant to attract mates of the same species. Male fireflies flash their beacons as they fly through the air. Females do not have wings. They flash a dimmer signal from the ground.

TERMITE

Like ants and bees, termites are social insects. They live in colonies that contain thousands of individuals. In tropical regions, termites build nests that tower high above the ground. In other areas, the colonies live underground or in fallen trees. Termites feed on dead trees and other rotting plants. They also like to munch on wooden buildings. Although termites are disliked by humans, they are very useful to the wildlife community. Termites loosen soil and clear dead wood from forest floors. This makes it easier for new plants to grow.

STINKBUG

Like many other animals, stinkbugs have an interesting method for protecting themselves from enemies. Whenever a stinkbug is threatened by an enemy, it freezes in a handstand pose. True to its name, the insect then releases a foul-smelling liquid from its abdomen. After getting a whiff of the nasty aroma, most enemies turn away in disgust. Many stinkbugs are brightly colored, so the other animal doesn't forget the unpleasant experience. The defense seems to work well. Most animals that have smelled one stinkbug never approach another.

FLEA

Fleas are tiny insects that live on humans and other animals. Unfortunately, blood is an adult flea's only source of food, which makes them very annoying guests. Fleas have bodies that are flattened from side to side. This allows them to run between the hairs of a host. Fleas also are hard and slippery, so they can escape scratching paws or pinching fingers. Once free, fleas leap away on their long, powerful legs. An average-sized flea can jump over the top of a shoe box. An equally gifted human, if one existed, could jump over the top of a football stadium!

LEAF INSECT

Among all animals, the leaf insect is the master of disguise. To avoid being eaten by birds and large insects, leaf insects have bodies that look like leaves. Their green, flattened bodies are even crisscrossed by leaflike veins. Some leaf insects also have patches of brown skin, similar to diseased leaves. Obviously, the disguise would not work well if leaf insects scurried up and down the trees they live on. As a result, the insects spend most of their lives sitting motionless. For exercise, they rock from side to side like leaves swaying in the breeze.

MANTIS

To other insects, mantises are the animals of nightmares. Unlike most other insects, mantises do not eat plants. They prefer to dine on living insects. Large mantises will even attack small frogs, lizards, and birds. Colored to match its surroundings, a mantis sits perfectly still, sometimes for hours. When a tasty snack strays too close, the mantis lunges forward and grabs the creature with its barbed forearms. The mantis usually eats its meal while the victim is still alive. After eating, the mantis washes its face much like a house cat.

CICADA

Like many other insects, cicadas spend most of their lives underground. After hatching from an egg, a young cicada, or *nymph*, burrows into the soil. The nymph's stay underground is no short affair; some species remain buried for 17 years! During this time, the nymph sucks juices from tree roots for nourishment. When the nymph finally surfaces, it's back splits open, and an adult cicada climbs out. The mature cicada lives for only five or six weeks. During this time, male cicadas blare out a loud, shrill call to attract females.

MONARCH BUTTERFLY

Among all insects, the monarch butterfly is the champion traveler. These orange-and-black butterflies spend summers in the northern United States and Canada. With the coming of autumn, the monarchs take to the skies. They fly south to avoid the cold northern winters. Several weeks later, the butterflies reach the mountains of southern Mexico, completing a journey of nearly 2,500 miles. In Mexico, millions of monarchs gather in tight, brilliant clusters. The butterflies rest during the winter, awaiting their return north in the spring.

COCKROACH

Cockroaches are the insect version of rats and mice. They live practically everywhere, though they prefer dark, moist crevices in houses, restaurants, and stores. At night, cockroaches come out of hiding and roam buildings in search of food. They use their long antennae to smell and feel their surroundings. Cockroaches eat nearly anything: scraps of food, stacks of paper, and even bindings on books. When surprised by light, cockroaches scamper away on their long, slender legs. To the surprise of many people, cockroaches also have wings and can fly.

WEEVIL

Equipped with trunklike snouts, weevils look like distant relatives of the elephant. Obviously, weevils are much smaller than elephants. In fact, some kinds of weevils are so small that they're hard to see.

Despite their small size, weevils are a nuisance to farmers. They damage crops throughout the world. Most weevils feed on plant stems, leaves, or roots. Others like to eat fruits or nuts. Weevil's mouths are located at the tip of their snouts. Armed with strong jaws and sharp teeth, weevils can chew through tough plant stems and even hard nutshells.